ARCHABET
An Architectural Alphabet

Photographs by Balthazar Korab

National Trust for Historic Preservation

THE PRESERVATION PRESS

FOREWORD

Like fine paintings and old friends, the best buildings are those that continually divulge surprises. Architectural surprises may be built in by the architect or builder, but at least half of the responsibility for finding pleasurable details in buildings rests firmly with us, the viewers and users. It is up to us to look for the delights that architecture offers beyond its larger role as shelter for our activities. And there are many ways of looking at architecture — through styles and materials, through form and function, through architects and history. One way to seek out the pleasures of buildings is to make a game of it. Here we have found an alphabet in architecture, seen through the eyes of an artist. This is only one way to view architecture, and only one of many alphabets that can be found hidden among the buildings that surround us, but it proves how rich even the simplest-seeming structures can be. To see architecture is to appreciate it, and to appreciate it is to want to save and savor those specimens that continue to give delight.

DIANE MADDEX

P R E F A C E

Under huge chestnut trees, in a formidable brick
school, I learned my ABCs from a teacher who
carved letters on the blackboard with squeaky chalk. Long
on the road since then, I have met other symbols from
other worlds: elegant white characters on a 15-story
red scroll on my Shanghai hotel, tiny wedge-shaped
Sumerian cuneiforms, arabesques caked with whitewash
on mosques in Yemen—all with messages, but not for me.
S.P.Q.R. inscribed in the streets of Rome, illuminated
medieval manuscripts, Rimbaud's colored poetry—these
still hold the most magic for me and are the alphabets of
my world. When converted to musical notation, letters
are charged with even richer emotional content. Indeed,
the basic purpose of the letter is to convert sound,
whether speech or music, into a visible mark. Letters have
been the link between two main motifs of the human
experience, reason and emotions. Thus, let our letters here
be the link between us and music of another kind:
the frozen music, architecture.

BALTHAZAR KORAB

What is architecture anyway? Is it the vast collection of the various buildings which have been built to please the varying tastes of the various lords of mankind? I think not. No, I know that architecture is life, or at least it is life itself taking form and therefore it is the truest record of life as it was lived in the world yesterday, as it is lived today or ever will be lived. So architecture I know to be a Great Spirit. It can never be something which consists of the buildings which have been built by man on earth. . . . Architecture is that great living creative spirit which from generation to generation, from age to age, proceeds, persists, creates, according to the nature of man, and his circumstances as they change. That is really architecture.

FRANK LLOYD WRIGHT

A

Learning to look is a pleasure;
the buildings will embrace your eyes.

Judith Lynch Waldhorn

B

Architecture begins where engineering ends.

WALTER GROPIUS

C

It is not enough to *see* architecture;
you must experience it.

Steen Eiler Rasmussen

D

The art of building, or architecture,
is the beginning of all the arts that lie
outside the person.

HAVELOCK ELLIS

E

Architecture, simply and
immediately perceived, is a combination,
revealed through light and shade,
of spaces, of masses, and of lines.

Geoffrey Scott

F

Architecture can reach out beyond
the period of its birth, beyond the social
class that called it into being,
beyond the style to which it belongs.

SIGFRIED GIEDION

G

All styles are good except the boring kind.

VOLTAIRE

H

Well-building hath three conditions:
Commodity, Firmness, and Delight.

Sir Henry Wotton

I

Ornament if organic was never
on the thing but *of* it. . . .

FRANK LLOYD WRIGHT

J

God is in the detail.

LUDWIG MIES VAN DER ROHE

K

Form ever follows function.

Louis Henri Sullivan

L

All architecture is shelter;
all great architecture is the design
of space that contains, cuddles, exalts,
or stimulates the persons in that space.

PHILIP JOHNSON

M

Consider . . . the momentous event
in architecture when the wall parted
and the column became.

<small>LOUIS I. KAHN</small>

N

We shape our buildings,
and afterwards our buildings shape us.

WINSTON S. CHURCHILL

Form is not the aim of our work, but only the result. Form, by itself, does not exist.

LUDWIG MIES VAN DER ROHE

P

When we build, let us think
that we build for ever.

John Ruskin

Less is more.

Ludwig Mies van der Rohe

R

I like complexity and contradiction
in architecture. . . . I am for messy vitality
over obvious unity. . . . I am for richness
of meaning rather than clarity of
meaning; for the implicit function
as well as the explicit function.

ROBERT VENTURI

S

I call architecture frozen music.

Johann Wolfgang von Goethe

T

Architecture is the masterly,
correct and magnificent play of volumes
brought together in light.

LE CORBUSIER

U

Architecture, like music, must be a part
of the composer, but it must also transcend
him to give something to music
or architecture itself. Mozart is not only
Mozart, but music.

Louis I. Kahn

V

We may live without her [architecture], and worship without her, but we cannot remember without her.

JOHN RUSKIN

W

One of modern architecture's greatest
failings has been its lack of interest
in the relationship of the building
to the sky. One doubts that a poem was
ever written to a flat-roofed building
silhouetted against the setting sun.

PAUL RUDOLPH

X

Architecture occurs when a building
and a person like each other.

WILLIAM WAYNE CAUDILL,
WILLIAM MERRIWEATHER PENA
and PAUL KENNON

Y

Architecture, unlike other arts,
is not an escape from, but an acceptance of,
the human condition, including its many
frailties as well as the technical advances
of its scientists and engineers.

PIETRO BELLUSCHI

Z

Let us, while waiting for new monuments,
preserve the ancient monuments.

Victor Hugo

ARCHABET

A Gothic Revival house,
Romeo, Mich.

B Sherman Minton Bridge over
the Ohio River between Louisville,
Ky., and New Albany, Ind.

C Interior of the cupola
at Longwood, Natchez, Miss.

D Good Luck gas station,
Dallas, Tex.

E Split rail fence
at Meffords Fort, Washington, Ky.

F Sawn-wood porch,
Monroe, Mich.

G Honolulu House,
Marshall, Mich.

H Donald Boudeman House,
Kalamazoo, Mich.

I Silos on a farm,
Monroe, Mich.

J Huntington House,
Howell, Mich.

K Abandoned gravel pit,
Oxford, Mich.

L Mitchell-Ogé House,
San Antonio, Tex.

M Rotunda of the Minnesota
State Capitol, St. Paul, Minn.

N Half-timbered house,
Old Salem, N.C.

O Gate near the Mississippi
River in Louisiana

P Lamp post at the Kingswood
School, Bloomfield Hills, Mich.

Q Windmill near a farmhouse,
Fenton, Mich.

R Sawyer House,
Monroe, Mich.

S Balcony grillwork
in the Vieux Carre,
New Orleans, La.

T Entrance portico
of the Cranbrook Art Academy,
Bloomfield Hills, Mich.

U Porch of the Tampa
Bay Hotel, Tampa, Fla.

V Old brick paving,
Savannah, Ga.

W Chapel of the Air
Force Academy,
Colorado Springs, Colo.

X Door of a house,
Monroe, Mich.

Y Gothic Revival house,
Washington, Ky.

Z Cast-iron stairway
in the City Hall,
Bay City, Mich.

QUOTATION SOURCES

Opening   "What Is Architecture." In *An Organic Architecture,* by Frank Lloyd Wright. 1939. 3rd ed. Cambridge: MIT Press, 1970.

A   *A Gift to the Street,* by Carol Olwell and Judith Lynch Waldhorn. 1976. Reprint. New York: St. Martin's Press, 1983.

B   Speech by Walter Gropius, Harvard Department of Architecture, 1938. See *Architects on Architecture: New Directions in America,* by Paul Heyer. 1966. Rev. ed. New York: Walker, 1978.

C   *Experiencing Architecture,* by Steen Eiler Rasmussen. Cambridge: MIT Press, 1959.

D   *The Dance of Life,* by Havelock Ellis. 1923. Reprint. Westport, Conn.: Greenwood Press, 1973.

E   *The Architecture of Humanism: A Study in the History of Taste,* by Geoffrey Scott. 1914, 1924. Reprint. New York: W. W. Norton, 1974.

F   *Space, Time and Architecture: The Growth of a New Tradition,* by Sigfried Giedion. Cambridge, Mass.: Harvard University Press, 1941.

G   "L'Enfant Prodigue," by Voltaire. 1736. In *Le Theatre de Voltaire,* edited by Theodore Besterman. Oxford: Voltaire Foundation, 1967.

H   After Vitruvius, *The Ten Books on Architecture,* Book 1, chapter iii. *The Elements of Architecture,* by Sir Henry Wotton. 1624. Reprint. Norwood, N.J.: Walter J. Johnson, 1970.

I   *A Testament,* by Frank Lloyd Wright. New York: Horizon Press, 1957.

J   Personal motto of Ludwig Mies van der Rohe. See "Mies van der Rohe," by Ludwig Glaeser. In *Macmillan Encyclopedia of Architects,* vol. 3, edited by Adolf K. Placzek. New York: Free Press, Macmillan, 1982.

K   "The Tall Office Building Artistically Considered," by Louis Henri Sullivan. *Lippincott's Magazine,* March 1896.

L   "What Makes Me Tick," speech by Philip Johnson, Columbia University, 1975. In *Philip Johnson: Writings.* New York: Oxford University Press, 1979.

M   *Between Silence and Light: Spirit in the Architecture of Louis I. Kahn,* by John Lobell. Boulder, Colo.: Shambhala Publications, 1979.

N   Speech by Winston S. Churchill, October 28, 1943. See *Winston S. Churchill: His Complete Speeches, 1897–1963,* edited by Robert Rhodes James. New York: Chelsea House, 1974.

O   Ludwig Mies van der Rohe, 1923. See *Mies van der Rohe,* by Werner Blaser. 1947. Rev. ed. New York: Praeger Publishers, 1978.

P   *The Seven Lamps of Architecture,* by John Ruskin. 1849. Reprint. New York: Farrar, Straus and Giroux, 1961.

Q   Personal motto of Ludwig Mies van der Rohe. See *Mies van der Rohe,* by Philip Johnson. 1947. New York: Museum of Modern Art, 1978.

R   *Complexity and Contradiction in Architecture,* by Robert Venturi. New York: Museum of Modern Art, 1966.

S   Letter from Goethe to Eckermann, February 4, 1829.

T   *Vers une Architecture,* by Le Corbusier. 1922. Paris: Arthaud, 1977.

U   *Between Silence and Light: Spirit in the Architecture of Louis I. Kahn,* by John Lobell. Boulder, Colo.: Shambhala Publications, 1979.

V   *The Seven Lamps of Architecture,* by John Ruskin. 1849. Reprint. New York: Farrar, Straus and Giroux, 1961.

W   "Paul Rudolph." In *Architects on Architecture: New Directions in America,* by Paul Heyer. 1966. Rev. ed. New York: Walker, 1978.

X   *Architecture and You: How to Experience and Enjoy Buildings,* by William Wayne Caudill, William Merriweather Pena and Paul Kennon. New York: Whitney Library of Design, 1978.

Y   "Pietro Belluschi." In *Architects on Architecture: New Directions in America,* by Paul Heyer. 1966. Rev. ed. New York: Walker, 1978.

Z   Victor Hugo, 1832.

The Preservation Press
National Trust for Historic Preservation
1785 Massachusetts Avenue, N.W.
Washington, D.C. 20036

The National Trust for Historic Preservation in the United States is the only private, nonprofit national organization chartered by Congress to encourage public participation in the preservation of sites, buildings and objects significant in American history and culture. Support is provided by membership dues, endowment funds, contributions and grants from federal agencies, including the U.S. Department of the Interior, under provisions of the National Historic Preservation Act of 1966. For information about membership and a complete list of other Preservation Press books, write to the National Trust at the above address.

ARCHABET was developed and edited by Diane Maddex, editor, Preservation Press books. Gretchen Smith, associate editor, and Helen Cook, administrative assistant, assisted with the production.

The book was designed by Marc Alain Meadows and Robert Wiser, Meadows & Wiser, Washington, D.C.

Type for the titles was composed in phototypositor Centaur by Phil's Photo, Inc., Washington, D.C., and for the text in Alphatype Centaurus by Harlowe Typography, Cottage City, Md. These typefaces were derived from a font designed by Bruce Rogers in 1915 for the Montague Press. The book was printed on 100-pound Mohawk Superfine by Wolk Press, Woodlawn, Md., and bound by Bookcrafters, Columbia, Md.

Printed in the United States of America

88 87 86 85   4 3 2 1

Library of Congress Cataloging in Publication Data

Korab, Balthazar.
    Archabet: an architectural alphabet.

    1. Buildings—United States—Pictorial
works.   2. Photography, Architectural.   I. Title.
NA705.K615 1985   779'.4'0924   84-26335
ISBN 0-89133-117-4